THE STRONG SAINT ABBA MOSES

SAINTS OF THE CHURCH SERIES

As Saint Gregory the Theologian said of Saint Athanasius, "In praising Athanasius, I shall be praising virtue. To speak of him and to praise virtue are identical, because he had, or, to speak more truly, has embraced virtue in its entirety. For all who have lived according to God still live unto God, though they have departed from here...Again, in praising virtue, I shall be praising God, Who gives virtue to men and lifts them up, or lifts them up again, to Himself by the enlightenment which is akin to Himself." Through this series, we desire not only to introduce the believers to the historical lives of the saints, but to recognize and praise the work of the Lord through them. By admiring the Light of the Lord shining brightly in and through them, we seek to develop our own personal relationship with God.

His Grace Bishop Serapion
Editor–in–Chief

Father Ishak Azmy Yacoub
Father John Paul Abdelsayed
Series Editors

BOOKS IN THIS SERIES

Saint Maurice and the Theban Legion
The Strong Saint Abba Moses
Saint Marina the Martyr
In Praise of Saint Paul

✝

Cⲩⲛ Ⲑⲉⲱ ⲓⲥⲭⲩⲣⲟⲥ

SAINTS OF THE CHURCH SERIES

The Strong Saint
Abba Moses

HERMIT, ABBOT, AND MARTYR

with a Preface by His Grace Bishop Serapion

Saint Paul Brotherhood Press

Coptic Orthodox Diocese of Los Angeles, Southern California, and Hawaii

THE STRONG SAINT ABBA MOSES

SAINT PAUL BROTHERHOOD PRESS

—∿—

Coptic Orthodox Diocese of Los Angeles, Southern California, and Hawaii

Saint Paul Brotherhood
38740 Avenida La Cresta
Murrieta, California 92562
www.SaintPaulBrotherhood.org

ISBN 978-0-9721698-3-7
LCCN 2014922768

"If a man's deeds are not in harmony with his prayer, he labors in vain."

— *Abba Moses*

His Holiness Pope Shenouda III

117th Pope and Patriarch of the
Great See of the City of Alexandria

His Grace Bishop Serapion

Bishop of the Coptic Orthodox Diocese of
Los Angeles, Southern California, and Hawaii

TABLE OF CONTENTS

PREFACE

The story of the life of the Strong Saint Abba Moses is a joyful story. I am pleased to present to you, dear readers, this valuable book about the life of Saint Moses the Ethiopian. I pray that Divine Grace may guide you through this joyful story to help you in your spiritual life.

I wish to reflect on five points regarding the life of Saint Moses the Black.

A MESSAGE OF HOPE

When we read the life of Saint Moses the Ethiopian we receive a message of hope. It is a story of conversion; a story of change about how a chief of a gang of seventy thieves became a head of a monastery of saintly monks; of a murderer who became a martyr; and the story of an adulterer who became a virgin. As it is said, "Repentance makes the adulterous virgins."

THE POWER OF REPENTANCE

Repentance is not an emotional feeling of regret over our sins; it is a change of mind, a *metanoia*. A change of mind above all means a change of behavior. In the life of Saint Moses the Ethiopian, there is a clear change of behavior.

I would like to highlight two stories in the life of Saint Moses the Ethiopian that demonstrate this change. Before his repentance and conversion, we read of his encounter with the shepherd:

He had as an enemy a certain shepherd, against whom he remembered certain evil things, and he went to steal sheep from his flock. The shepherd was told by a certain man, "Moses has crossed the Nile by swimming, and he holds a sword in his hand, and his clothes are placed on his head, and he has crossed the river by swimming." The shepherd entirely covered himself with sand and hid from him. When Moses came and did not find the shepherd, he chose out two fine rams from the sheep, slew them, tied them together with a rope, and swam across the river with them. Having come to a small village, he skinned the rams and ate the best portions of them. He sold the remainder for wine and drank. After these things he went back to his companions.

The other story happened after his conversion, and demonstrates the change which happened in his life, in his attitude, and in his mind.

About him they tell the story that [four] thieves once came to him and went into his cell, because they did not know who he was. He tied them all together with cords and lifted them up on his shoulders like a bag of chopped straw. He brought them to the brethren in the church, and said to the brethren, "Since I have not the power to do evil to any man, what do you command me to do to those who rose up against me to slay me?" Now at that time Moses had been fasting for seven days, and he had eaten nothing. After he had done this he informed the thieves, saying, "I indeed am Moses who was formerly the captain of a band of thieves."

Having heard this, they praised and glorified God. When they saw the sincerity of his repentance they also removed themselves from their evil deeds, and said within themselves, "Let us also draw near to repentance, so that we may become worthy of the forgiveness of sins, even as he also is worthy."

REPENTANCE IS A LIFELONG STRUGGLE FOR HOLINESS

Repentance is not a momentary change; it is a struggle for holiness that lasts throughout one's whole life. In the life of Saint Moses the Black we discover a clear *metanoia* in his life. This change was a beginning; it was not an end. After his repentance, he had to struggle against temptation against the Devil. In his life, we read:

> While fasting often, and during the time of prayer and silent contemplation, that devil of error, who brings back to the remembrance of the mind the wickedness of former habits, would come to him, and tempt him to such a degree that, even as he himself has told us, he wanted exceedingly little to make Moses fall from his covenant.

He used to go to his father of confession, Saint Isidore, to tell him about his struggle. His father of confession told him,

> Do not be distressed, for these are the beginning of the birth pangs, and they come upon you seeking what they are accustomed to receive. When a dog comes continually to the cook, if a man gives him nothing he will not go there again. Thus also it is with you: for if you will continue in fasting, in prayer, and in silent contemplation, the Devil will

immediately fall into despair and will flee from you.

We often hear complaints from people that they fell again after they repented. They think that repentance is a momentary change, after which the Devil will not return to attack and tempt them. But the story of Saint Moses the Ethiopian tells us that repentance is a beginning of struggle. We should not give up; we should not be distressed. Rather, we have to continue. The Devil will come, time and again. But if we reject his tricks and his devices, he will not return, as in the example of the dog mentioned by Saint Isidore.

THE VICTORIOUS LIFE IS THE GIFT OF DIVINE GRACE

We learn from the story of Saint Moses the Ethiopian that repentance and the life of holiness is not only our work as human beings, but also a gift of Divine Grace. His struggle was very ascetic. He fasted; he journeyed to help the other monks; and he performed numerous ascetic works. But his father of confession, Saint Isidore, said to him:

> Rest yourself, O Moses. Do not trouble yourself against the devils, and do not seek to make attacks on them. 'There is moderation in everything, even in the works of ascetic life.'

And he assured him saying,

> In the Name of Jesus Christ, from this time forward the devils shall cease from you. Draw near, then, and participate in the Holy Mysteries, and you shall be free from all impurity both of the flesh and of the spirit. You must not boast within yourself, and say, 'I have overcome the devils,' for it

was for your benefit that they have waxed strong against you. So Moses returned again to his cell. After two months, Abba Isidore came to him and asked him concerning himself. Moses said to him, "I never see now anything which is hateful to me." Now he was also held to be worthy of the gift of Divine Grace.

So, in our repentance, we have to struggle. But we have to know that the victorious life is not our action; it is a gift from above. When God sees our sincere desire to struggle for a life of holiness, He will grant us, as Divine Grace granted Saint Moses the Ethiopian, rest from the continuous attacks of the Devil.

THE IMPORTANCE OF THE FATHER OF CONFESSION

The life of Saint Moses the Ethiopian shows us the importance of the father of confession. Through his life, he was supported by a great father of confession, Saint Isidore. He received Moses when he came to the wilderness of Shiheet. He helped Moses to know the Christian faith. He led Moses in his repentance, and guided him in his first confession. He helped him through his struggle. He guided him how to be strong against the temptation of the Devil, not to boast within himself, and how to depend on Divine Grace. He guided him, on the one hand, in the ascetic life with moderation, and on the other, in the spiritual life, participating in the Holy Mysteries, praying, and asking God to help him.

So, in our struggle and repentance, we need guidance. Therefore, our church arranged for every believer to be guided by his father of confession and to be a true disciple of his father of confession.

Again, I am pleased to present to you this book about Saint Moses the Ethiopian, which gives to each one of us joy and hope, shows us the power of repentance, teaches us that repentance is a struggle of our life, and warns us not to depend on ourselves, but to depend on Divine Grace to grant us the gift of victorious life under the direction of our father of confession.

May our Lord Jesus Christ bless this book for the glory of His Name through the intercession of the Strong Saint Abba Moses.

Glory be to the Holy Trinity, our God, unto the Ages of all ages, Amen.

Bishop Serapion
Feast of the Strong Saint Abba Moses
1 July 2010 A.D.
24 Paouna 1726 A.M.

I

INTRODUCTION

On the mountain of Shiheet[1] shined a brilliant star to whom is due magnificent glorification and doxology, Saint Moses the Ethiopian. Out of the merciful God's extraordinary goodness he was called from an utterly abominable manner of living in the world to the most perfect life of holiness in the desert. Consequently, it can truly be said of him that he was a prodigy of God's grace who deserves our admiration and a most mighty adoration from those living a profoundly sinful life that they may return to God with contrite heart.

Saint Moses the Ethiopian is commemorated in the Coptic rite on 24 Paouna (July 1 in Gregorian Calendar). The Ethiopian Orthodox Church commemorates his feast on 24 Sane in the Ethiopian calendar, which coincides with June 17.[2] The Eastern Orthodox (Old Calendarists), Roman

---

[1] Originally in Coptic, "Shiheet" (ϢⲒⲀⲎⲦ) which means "the balance or measure of the hearts." In Arabic it became known as Wadi El Natroun (the Nitrian Valley) because of the eight different nitrate lakes in the region. In Greek, it was translated as Scetis from which the English word is derived for the ascetics who used to dwell there. The original Coptic "Shiheet" is used throughout this book.

[2] Job Ludolf, *Fastis Sacris Ecclesiae Aethiopicae*, p. 419 and n. i.

and Eastern Catholic, and Anglican churches venerate Saint Moses on August 27 or 28. The Eastern Orthodox churches that follow the New Calendar commemorate Saint Moses on September 10.

HISTORICAL SOURCES

The principal account of the life of Saint Moses comes from Palladius' *Lausiac History,* The details that two Greek-language biographies (of which there are extant transcripts) recall concerning the saint are generally ascribed to Palladius. One of these accounts comes from a manuscript of the Imperial Library in Vienna, although no author is mentioned. Papebroch left us another transcript from MS. Ambros. f. N. n. 152. There is also an account found in the *Bibliotheca Sanctorum* by J. W. Sauget and approximately 49 apophthegmata in *The Desert Christian* compiled by Sister Benedicta Ward. The *Acta Sanctorum* contains a Latin translation of the Greek, with various notes on the *Life,* upon which we have relied much.[3] We are most grateful to Professor Edward Strickland who translated this work from Latin, as well as Brother Cassian Di Rocco, O.S.B of the Roman Catholic Church, and Brother Angelos of Saint Mary and Saint Moses Abbey in the Coptic Orthodox Diocese of the Southern United States for assisting in this process.

CHRONOLOGY OF HIS LIFE

The life of Saint Moses is well documented. The *Lausiac History* and a copy of the *Vita*[4] from the Imperial Library in

---

[3] "Saint Moses the Ethiopian: Hermit, Abbot, and Perhaps Martyr at Mt. Scetis in Libya, Introduction and Commentary," *Acta Sanctorum,* August VI, pp. 199-209.

[4] The *Vita's* explicit is: τελευτᾷ δὲ ἐτῶν ἑβδομήκοντα πέντε ἐν τῇ Σκήτῃ.

Vienna confirm he lived to the age of seventy-five years.[5] As far as the historical documents allow us, we will attempt to provide a systematic chronology the events in the life of this great saint of the desert.

If Saint Moses finished his life at the end of the fourth century, we can posit that his life began around 325. Tillemont indicates that his conversion occurred when he was twenty-five or thirty years old, that is, from 350 or 355.[6] According to Baillet, Abba Moses was the hegumen, or the spiritual director of a monastery of solitaries in Shiheet, some time between 375 or 380. Specifying the year of his death, however, is more difficult. It is beyond doubt that our saint departed before 420, when Palladius spoke of his death.[7] Some approximate his departure between 391 or 392, when Palladius may have spoken with him, and 400, when John Cassian most probably left Egypt.[8]

OTHER SAINTS CALLED MOSES

The Greek *Life of our Holy Father Moses the Ethiopian* provides the famous title for our saint: Moses the Ethiopian. Its incipit is: "This blessed Moses was, in fact, of Ethiopian

---

γεγονὼς καὶ πρεσβύτερος, καταλιπὼν ἐβδμήκοντα μαθητάς. Ταῖς πρεσβείαις αὐτοῦ, Κύριε, σῶσον πάντας ἡμᾶς, etc… Which means "He died at the age of seventy-five at Shiheet; he had been made a priest and left behind seventy disciples. Through his intercession, Lord, save us all, etc…"

[5] Palladius, *Historia Lausiaca,* 35. On the contrary, Nicephorus Callistus asserts that he lived to the age of eighty-five. Nicephorus Callistus, *Ecclesiasticae historiae,* 11.36 in vol. 2.

[6] Tillemont, *Monumentorum ecclesiasticorum,* 10, p. 64.

[7] *Ibid.,* p. 75.

[8] John Cassian, *Collationes,* 3.5, 7.26.

nationality and completely black in color."[9] Due to his African background, he is also referred to, in some of the sayings and histories, as "Saint Moses the Black." In the Commemoration of Saints in the Coptic Liturgies attributed to Saint Basil and Saint Cyril, he is called "The Strong Saint Abba Moses" (Ⲡⲓⲭⲱⲣⲓ ⲉⲑⲟⲩⲁⲃ Ⲁⲃⲃⲁ Ⲙⲱⲥⲏ; and in the similar prayer in the Divine Liturgy attributed to Saint Gregory, he is called "the Strong Abba Moses" (Ⲡⲓⲭⲱⲣⲓ Ⲁⲃⲃⲁ Ⲙⲱⲥⲏ)

In the accounts of the desert fathers and saints, six other references to a father by the name of Moses are found. The first three below most probably are *not* the same saint as Moses the Ethiopian; however it is likely that most or all of the latter three are the same individual. Unfortunately, we cannot decisively conclude whether all of these refer to the same Saint Moses without more historical evidence.

1) **Saint Moses, bishop of the Saracens in Arabia.**[10] He was apparently first a solitary before being ordained bishop and lived around 375. While it is true, that the title "Saracen" could be applied to the nomadic Bedouins in the Middle East, including Syria, Nubia and Ethiopia, there is no mention in the other literature that Abba Moses the Ethiopian was ordained a bishop; but he departed in Shiheet.

2) **Moses (Moisees) the Martyr** (Mesra 26 in Coptic calendar; September 1 in the Gregorian calendar; and August 19 in the Julian calendar). He was martyred with his sister, Sarah. According to the Coptic Synaxarium, he

---

[9] Οὗτος ὁ μακάριος Μωσῆς τῷ μὲν γένει ἦν Αἰθίοψ. τῇ χροίᾳ μέλας κριβῶς.

[10] *Acta Sanctorum,* February, 2, p. 45.

entered into one of the monasteries and there remained for 10 years before his martyrdom. This saint is probably not the same saint as Saint Moses the Ethiopian because latter most probably spent a longer time in the monastery. Also, the other accounts mention nothing of his sister. Instead, Abba Moses the Ethiopian, if martyred, was martyred with other monks in the monastery.

3) **Saint Moses of Abydos.** This Abba Moses lived at and founded a monastery at Abydos in the sixth century. Today, the monastic settlement is still in used, and referred to as *Dayr Bakhūm* or *Dayr al-Rum*.[11] The stories of Abba Moses of Abydos are preserved in two manuscripts originally from the White Monastery, i.e. the Monastery of Saint Shenoute. Despite our knowledge of Moses, he has no entry in the Alexandrian Synaxarium on his feast day, 25 Abib (1 August).[12] However, the Synaxarium does explain many events in his life, as well as the flourishing of his monastery after his departure.

4) **Saint Moses of Lybia.** There is also another saint called Saint Moses of Libya who was martyred in Egypt with six monk martyrs.[13] He is recorded giving seven instructions

---

[11] "Abydos," in *The Coptic Encyclopedia*, 1st ed.; see also Mark Moussa, "The Coptic Literary Dossier of Abba Moses of Abydos," *Coptic Church Review* 24:3 (2003):66-90; idem., "Abba Moses of Abydos," (MA Diss, Catholic University of America, 1998); Rene Georges Coquin, "Etudes sur Moise d'Abydos," *Annuaire de l'Ecolepratique des Hautes Etudes, Ve section, Sciences religieuses* (1983/84): 373-376; idem., "Moise d'Abydos," *Deuxiéme journee detudes coptes, Cahiers de la bibliotheque copte* 3 (1986):1-14.; idem., "La 'Règle' de Moise d'Abydos," *Cahiers d'Orientalisme* 20 (1988): 103-110.

[12] Moussa, p. 67.

[13] *Ibid.*, p. 46.

to Abba Poemen.[14] Palladius wrote of him that he "was an extremely mild man endowed with the utmost charity. He was considered a worthy recipient of the gift of healing."[15] Sozomen wrote that he "had fame greater than others and is remembered for his meekness, his charity, his tending to people's weariness, ills over which his prayers alone were efficacious."[16] Scholars are divided whether this Moses is the same as our Abba Moses the Ethiopian.

Unfortunately, Palladius does not recount the departures of Moses of Ethiopia and Moses of Libya, but simply witnesses that Moses of Ethiopia "became an elder." Some scholars posited that the account of Saint Moses' martyrdom coincides with Saint Moses of Ethiopia's past life of robbery and murder. As Saint Moses of Libya recounts in a concluding passage, "For so many years have I awaited this day that the word that my Lord Jesus Christ said be fulfilled, 'All that take the sword shall perish with the sword.'"

While scholarship is generally inconclusive, the Coptic rite has traditionally equated the two as one. The Ethiopian tradition also records seven brothers martyred with "Abba Moses the Black."[17]

---

[14] *Ibid.*, 6.4, p. 657; 7.1, p. 678; see *Acta Sanctorum*, February 7, p. 47; Rosweyde, 109, p. 1007; Cotelier, pp. 555, 557, 816; *Vitae Patrum* 5.10.63, p. 602.

[15] Palladius, 88, p. 184.

[16] Sozomen, *Historia ecclesiastica*, 6.29, p. 684.

[17] In the *Fastis Sacris Ecclesiae Aethiopicae*, June 17 commemorates "Abba Moses the Black and of the seven brothers of Moses the Black." Ludolf, p. 419 and n.i.

5) **Moses of Shiheet.** This Abba Moses is mentioned by
John Cassian in his *Conferences.*[18] Some historians argue that
Moses of Shiheet cannot be Saint Moses of Ethiopia, either
because the latter is much older than Cassian[19] or because
Moses of Shiheet is much younger than Saint Moses the
Ethiopian who was with Saint Antony from his youth.[20]
However, Tillemont provides evidence that Saint Moses of
Ethiopia must have lived up until 390, when Cassian came
to visit Shiheet.[21] Furthermore, this Moses must have lived
to an even later date, since Cassian above all recognized
Moses' virtue, that he had withdrawn into solitude as a result
of the brigandage that he had committed, and that he had
lived in a place named Calamus in the desert of Shiheet.[22]
Most probably, the Moses who lived in Calamus is the same
one in Cassian's *Conferences*, and the famous Moses the ex-
robber of whom one reads in the *Vitae Patrum* and *Lausiac
History*[23] However, this is still a matter of great debate.

6) **Moses of Nitria.** This Moses is mentioned with Abba
Poemen the anchorite and resembles both Saint Moses the
Ethiopian and Moses of Libya.[24] Again, this is inconclusive,

[18] Tillemont, *Monumentorum ecclesiasticorum,* 10.

[19] *Ibid.*, p. 218 nn; Alard Gazet, ed., *Collationes 1: Joannis Cassiani opera omnia* (Paris: 1642).

[20] Louis Bulteau, *Histoire de l'ordre monastique,* 1.10, p. 154.

[21] Tillemont, p. 728 n. 3 (on S. Moses the ex-robber).

[22] See the text that we cited above in § 1.5.

[23] Tillemont, p. 218. The *Vitae Patrum* also mentions seventy disciples
who followed the great father Abba Moses. Many of the sayings mention
two of his disciples: Zacharias and Carion. This evidence demonstrates
that they dwelt in Shiheet, in the same region under Isidore the priest, or
"Isidore the Great." Tillemont, p. 76; *Vitae Patrum* 3.86, p. 513, 5.15.17.
p. 623; Cotelier, pp. 443-44, 516.

[24] Tillemont, p. 26.

since we lack details from his life. Once again, we cannot conclusively determine whether he is the same as Abba Moses the Ethiopian, since we lack details from the life of the former. However, the location of the two saints is similar, since Nitria was the famous mountain bordering Shiheet.

II

HIS LIFE AND CONVERSION

In the *Lausiac History* we read, "There was a black man named Moses who was by nationality Ethiopian."[1] He was also tall, or to use Rosweyde's word, *longus?*[2] He followed a contemptible, criminal way of life. According to Sozomen: "Although he was a slave, Moses was expelled from his master's house because of his wickedness; he turned to a life of brigandage and rose to become a leader of a band of thieves."[3]

Palladius wrote that he was "the slave of a state official." He mentions his egregious acts of unbridled barbarism and abominable crimes. By the Grace of God, Moses turned from this sullied course of life by means of true repentance, with a contrite and humble heart which God's mercy does not despise. Palladius said, "This prince of thieves was ultimately in the latter portion of his life brought to feel compunction in virtue of some disaster that befell him, and took himself to a monastery."[4] In this way, he achieved a

---

[1] Palladius, *Historia Lausiaca*, 22 (Paris, 1570), p. 62.

[2] *Vitae Patrum,* trans. by Heribert Rosweyde, 2nd ed., 5.8.10, p. 593.

[3] Sozomen, *Historia ecclesiastica* 6.29, trans. by Henri Valois (Paris, 1668), p. 682.

[4] Palladius, p. 63.

remarkable degree of holiness.

While Palladius tells us that Saint Moses repented and went to the monastery because "some disaster fell on him" (p. 63), unfortunately neither Palladius nor Sozomen explain what this misfortune was. It seems to be different from the circumstance we read in the appendix to the *Vitae Patrum* or to indicate something different from what the aforementioned authors understood. Neither Palladius or Sozomen's reference to a "certain misfortune" in the life of Abba Moses prove this was his intended manner of converting. Contrary to the earlier account, John Cassian, recorded the following:

> There was, in fact, nothing wanting in Abba Moses' observance (he dwelt in a locale of that wilderness called Calamus); it was such as merits perfect blessedness. For fear of the death that loomed over him on account of his having committed murder, he was driven to hasten to a monastery. He felt so strongly a need to convert that in consequence of his heart's ready virtue that he transformed a feeling into an act of the will and attained to the very heights of perfection.[5]

HIS LIFE IN THE *VITAE PATRUM*[6]

Now there was a certain man whose name was Moses, who was by race an Ethiopian. His skin was black and he was the slave of a man in high authority. Because of his evil deeds and thefts, his master drove him out of his house. Now it is said that he even went so far as to commit murder.

---

[5] John Cassian, *Collationes*, 3.5 (Lyons, 1606), p. 221.
[6] *Vitae Patrum*, 2.10.

People say concerning him that he was even the captain of a band of seventy thieves. Now I am compelled to mention his wickedness so that I may show the beauty of his repentance. The following thing used to be related about him, and he is said to have committed it during the period in which he passed his time in stealing.

He had as an enemy a certain shepherd, against whom he remembered certain evil things, and he went to steal sheep from his flock. The shepherd was told by a certain man, "Moses has crossed the Nile by swimming, and he holds a sword in his hand, and his clothes are placed on his head, and he has crossed the river by swimming." The shepherd entirely covered himself with sand and hid from him. When Moses came and did not find the shepherd, he chose out two fine rams from the sheep, slew them, tied them together with a rope, and swam across the river with them. Having come to a small village, he skinned the rams and ate the best portions of them. He sold the remainder for wine and drank. After these things he went back to his companions.

One day, while he was associated with them in doing hateful things, his senses returned to him in the morning and he repented of his evil acts. He rose up and fled to a monastery. From that time he drew near to works of repentance so closely that the demon who had made him sin since his youth, and who desired to continue to make him sin, would stand before him in visible form and would look on him. Thus, he came to the knowledge of our Lord Christ.

About him they tell the story that [four] thieves once came to him and went into his cell, because they did not know who he was. He tied them all together with cords and lifted them up on his shoulders like a bag of chopped straw. He brought them to the brethren in the church, and said to the brethren, "Since I have not the power to do evil to any man, what do you command me to do to those who rose up against me to slay me?" Now at that time Moses had been fasting for seven days, and he had eaten nothing. After he had done this he informed the thieves, saying, "I indeed am Moses who was formerly the captain of a band of thieves." Having heard this, they praised and glorified God. When they saw the sincerity of his repentance they also removed themselves from their evil deeds, and said within themselves, "Let us also draw near to repentance, so that we may become worthy of the forgiveness of sins, even as he also is worthy."

While fasting often, and during the time of prayer and silent contemplation, that devil of error, who brings back to the remembrance of the mind the wickedness of former habits, would come to him, and tempt him to such a degree that, even as he himself has told us, he wanted exceedingly little to make Moses fall from his covenant. Having come to the old man[7] Isidore the Great, who had arrived from Shiheet, Moses told him concerning the war of his body. The old man said to him, "Do not be distressed, for these are the beginning of the birth pangs, and they come upon you seeking what they are accustomed to receive. When a dog comes continually to the cook, if a man gives him nothing he will not go there again. Thus also it is with you: for if you will continue in fasting, in prayer, and in silent contemplation, the Devil will immediately fall into despair and will flee from you."

---

[7] In the Bohairic dialect of the Coptic Language, "old man" or elder is the same word for "monk." — ϧⲉⲗⲗⲱ.

From that time he was exceedingly constant in his work of spiritual excellence. He ate nothing whatsoever except ten [or twelve] ounces of dry bread daily when he was doing work. He would recite fifty prayers from beginning to end during the day, but the more he dried up his body, the more he was vexed and consumed by dreams. Again he went to one of the old men, and said to him, "What shall I do? For thoughts of lust which arise from my former habits attack me." The old man said to him, "These lead you into error because you have not turned away your heart from the likes of them. Give your heart to vigil and careful prayer and you will be free from them."

Now when he had heard this direction, he went to his cell and made a covenant with God that he would neither sleep during the entire night nor bend his knees. He dwelt in his cell for seven years, and remained standing the entirety of each night with his eyes open; he never closed his eyelids. After this, he set for himself other ascetic labors. He would go out during the night, visit the cells of the old men,[8] take their water-skins and fill them with water, because they lived a long way from the water—that is to say, some two miles, some four miles, and others five miles. One night, he went to fill the water-skins with water, according to his custom.

When he had bent down over the spring, a devil smote him a blow across his loins as with a stick, and then departed leaving him halfdead. But Moses understood who had done this thing to him.

On the following day, one of the brethren came to fill the water skins with water. When he saw he blessed man

---

[8] That is, the elder monks.

lying there, he drew near to him and asked him, "What has happened to you?" After Moses told him the story, the brother went and informed Abba Isidore, the priest of the church of Shiheet. Abba Isidore immediately sent brethren and they took him up and brought him to the church. He was ill for a long time. He never thoroughly recovered from his illness, and he never again enjoyed the health of body of which he had possessed formerly.

Abba Isidore said to him, "Rest yourself, O Moses. Do not trouble yourself against the devils, and do not seek to make attacks on them. There is moderation in everything, even in the works of ascetic life." Then Moses said to him, "I believe in God, in Whom I have placed my hope, that being armed against the devils I must not cease to wage war with them until they depart from me." And Abba Isidore said to him, "In the Name of Jesus Christ, from this time forward the devils shall cease from you. Draw near, then, and participate in the Holy Mysteries, and you shall be free from all impurity both of the flesh and of the spirit. You must not boast within yourself, and say, 'I have overcome the devils,' for it was for your benefit that they have waxed strong against you." So Moses returned again to his cell. After two months, Abba Isidore came to him and asked him concerning himself. Moses said to him, "I never see now anything which is hateful to me."

Now he was also held to be worthy of the gift of Divine Grace, and he could chase away the devils from many people who were vexed with them. As flies take to flight before us, so the devils departed from before him. Such were the ascetic labors of the blessed man Moses, who was himself vexed with great matters. He also became a priest, and he left behind him seventy disciples who were men of worth. When he was a thief he had as followers seventy men who were thieves, and these now became his disciples, and they were perfect in the fear of God.

APPENDIX TO HIS LIFE [9]

Neither slaves nor evildoers are excluded from the Kingdom of God. Rather, within it are those who have, as they have need, experienced conversion, who have chosen to live correctly and in accord with God. Assuredly, neither Scythians nor Ethiopians are excluded from the Kingdom of God. Everyone has, in fact, a capacity of belonging to Christ's flock. Christ, the Good Shepherd, draws everyone to the fold of knowledge and lays down His life on behalf of the sheep. One can observe this from the lives of many others, but especially from that of the subject whose life is now our topic to narrate: I mean Moses the Ethiopian. In point of fact, as disordered a man as he had been, so great and renowned has he become for his virtue.

Moses was a man who had a body that was dark black, but had a soul that shone brighter than the brilliance of the sun. He was the domestic slave of a magistrate;[10] he was not well behaved as a domestic and did not give thought to what was pleasing to his master. To the contrary, his mind was on what was greatly opposed to good conduct. In fact, whatever at all was base, promiscuous, disordered, or beyond the pale of acceptable conduct[11] is what he did, what he thought of, what he had, so to speak, in his hands and in his mind every

---

[9] *Vitae Patrum,* 2.10.

[10] Πολιτευσένου—probably a typographical error for πολιτευμνου. Cf. Du Cange, *Glossarium graecitatis* 2, s.v., which cites this very passage with the second form.

[11] ἀπειρημνου—literally, "not to be tried or undertaken."

day. Moses was completely undeflected from his intention by his master's wrath, by the punishment he dispensed, and the other forms of ill-treatment he was made to suffer. His master, consequently, gave up on correcting him; his benefactor went further and drove him from his sight. Moses began to keep company with brigands, thieves, murderers, and every other class of criminal. It is worthwhile to mention one episode from this period.

Relying on his bodily strength, Moses once went out alone to rob. So, since a shepherd hindered him and thwarted his assault—whether he did so by informing on him or some other means I cannot say—Moses went completely mad. During the night he swam across the Nile, which was then at its flood stage, and attacked him. Since the shepherd was aware of his approach before his arrival and turned to flight, Moses did not attain his goal. In his rage, he slaughtered four choice rams, tied them up with a cord, and traversed the river with them. So, he consumed their meat, sold their furs for wine, and caught up with his companions, who lived about fifty stadia[12] from the river. These terrible acts of delinquency,[13] and worse than these, were characteristic of Moses. I have gone over these deeds and all the while have been astounded at God's compassion and forbearance for His own image, how He draws everyone to salvation by means of repentance, how nothing exists that is so wicked that it could prevail over His grandeur and indescribable mercy.

Indeed, Moses was a leader of brigands of such great renown that even the mention of his name instilled fear in

---

[12] Approximately 6.25 miles.

[13] νεανιεύματα καὶ τεκνάσματα.

many. He was notorious for his wickedness and unrivaled in harshness. God's grace touched his soul for a reason not at all inconsiderable. By the instrumentality of grace, Moses underwent a sudden change and became mindful of God, death, and judgment. He utterly abandoned that long-practiced occupation of his—an occupation fraught with sin, and forsook any connection with desert ambushes and lairs.

He unexpectedly approached a monastery; his aspect was pitiful out of reverence for the ascetics. His manner was humble; his spirit shuddered. He was speechless,[14] wrought with emotion, tearful, and continually groaning. Initially, he engendered fear in the monks who dwelt there. Then, he fell at the feet of the hegumen[15] and warmly asked for pardon for his acts of wrongdoing. He recited them down to the last detail. He declared his disordered thoughts and deeds, his reflections and intentions, and his activities. He left none of what he had done unsaid. Indeed, because these deeds needed forgiveness his intention was that none should go unadmitted.

To combat these he asked of those who had utterly renounced the world that he receive the guarantee of salvation, I mean the monastic habit. He then poured out copious tears that his desire not be denied; he prostrated himself and pleaded with them. Then, the hegumen was astonished by the incredible nature of his transformation. When he had heard of his doings, he welcomed him kindly, gave him a kiss, grasped both his hands, and raised him up as if he were someone great.

---

[14] καταφής.

[15] This most probably refers to Abba Isidore of Shiheet.

THE CALL OF GOD INTO THE LIFE OF GRACE [16]

The brethren asked, "In how many ways does Divine Grace call the brethren to the life of the solitary ascetic?" The old man said, "In many different ways. Sometimes, Divine Grace moves a man suddenly, as it moved Abba Moses the Ethiopian; sometimes by the hearing of the Scriptures, as in the cases of the blessed Abba Anthony and Abba Simon the Stylite; and at others fathers by the doctrine of the Word, as in the cases of Serapion, Abba Bessarion, and others like to them. Concerning these three ways by which Divine Grace calls to those who would repent, I would say that Divine Grace moves the conscience of a monk in the manner which is pleasing to God. Through these, even evildoers repented and pleased God. Moreover, there is the departure from this world by the hands of angels; by terrors, sicknesses, and afflictions. And sometimes, God Himself calls from heaven and takes a man out of the world, as in the cases of Paul and Abba Arsenius.

[16] *Vitae Patrum*, 2.657.

III

A LIFE OF SOLITUDE

We follow the holy man into the solitude of Shiheet, which fostered the observances of some outstanding solitaries. As explained above, we are not absolutely certain that the below sayings can all be attributed to Abba Moses the Ethiopian.

Pursue Tranquility[1]

Abba Moses said to Abba Macarius in Shiheet, "I wish to live in tranquility and silence, but the brethren do not allow me." Abba Macarius said to him, "I see that you have a difficult disposition and are unable to turn a brother away. But if you long for a tranquil life, set out for the inner desert in Petra. You will live in tranquility there." So he did, and he acquired profound tranquility.

Flee the World[2]

A man who flees from other men is like a ripe grape, but he who dwells among the attractions of the children of men is like a sour grape.

---

[1] Jean-Baptiste Cotelier, *Ecclesiae Graecae Monumenta,* p. 538.

[2] *Vitae Patrum* 5.2.10, p. 564; *Paradise,* Book I, vol. 1, §35.

Your Cell Will Teach You[3]

A certain brother went to Abba Moses in Shiheet and asked him to speak a word. The old man said to him, "Go and sit in your cell, and your cell will teach you everything, if you stay there. Indeed, just as a fish out of water dies immediately, so, too, a monk perishes if his object is to loiter outside his cell."

Silence[4]

Once, the fathers of Shiheet were gathered together. Because some people wanted to see Abba Moses, [some fathers] treated him rudely saying, "Why does this Ethiopian come and go in our midst?" But Moses, upon hearing this, held his peace. When the congregation was dismissed, they said to him, "Abba Moses, were you not upset?" And he said to them, "Although I was upset, I did not utter a word."

The Exaltation of the Just[5]

When a certain brother in Shiheet was going to the harvest, he went to Abba Moses the Black[6] and said to him, "Father, tell me what I shall do: should I go to the harvest?" Abba Moses said to him, "If I tell you, will listen and do as I

---

[3] *Vitae Patrum* 3.109, p. 516; *Paradise,* Book I, vol. 1, §62.

[4] *Paradise,* Book I, vol. 2, Ch 1, §55.

[5] *Paradise,* Book I, vol. 2, Ch 1, §18; *Vitae Patrum,* 3.102, p. 516;
Sozomen, *Historia ecclesiastica* 6.29, trans. Henri Valois (Paris, 1668), p. 682.

[6] The same story is told in the Sayings of the Desert Fathers, although without reference to Abba Moses. See Benedicta Ward, *The Desert Fathers: Sayings of the Early Christian Monks,* (London: Penguin Books Ltd, 2003), p. 144.

say?" And the brother said to him, "Yes, I will listen to you." The old man said to him, "If you will listen to me, get up, go, and release yourself from going to the harvest. Come to me and I will tell you what to do." So, the brother departed and excused himself from his friends, as the old man had told him. Then he came to Abba Moses and he said to him, "Go into your cell and keep the Pentecost. You shall eat dry bread and salt once a day only. After you have done this, I will tell you something else to do."

He went and did as the old man had told him, then came to him again. Now when the old man saw that he was one who worked with his hands, he showed him the proper way to live in his cell. The brother went to his cell, fell on the ground and wept before God for three whole days and nights.

After these things, when his thoughts were saying to him, "You are now an exalted person and you have become a great man," he used to contradict them and focus on his past weaknesses, saying, "So were all your sins." And when they used to say to him, "You have performed many things negligently," he would say, "Nevertheless I do small services for God and He has mercy on me." When these spirits were conquered in this way, they appeared to him in the form of bodily creatures and said to him, "We have been defeated by you." And he said to them, "Why?" And they said to him, "If we humble you, you raise us up; and if we exalt you, you humble us."

IV

A LIFE OF STRUGGLE

Our indefatigable athlete endured many contests: wicked temptations of the flesh in such great number and severity did not harm him. Thus, his soul found its glory in the grand profusion of heavenly rays that bathed it and he wielded a wondrously potent empire over demons, as witnesses Palladius: "Indeed, this saint was granted grace over demons; to the extent that we disregard flies in winter, so did this great man Moses—no, even more did he despise demons."[1] In fact, the holy man struck the most profound terror in demons.

Do Not Worry[2]

They used to say of Abba Moses in Shiheet that when he was going to Petra[3] he became weary on the way; he said

---

[1] Palladius, p. 66.

[2] *Paradise of the Fathers,* Book I, vol. 1, §62.

[3] Petra (or Patra) here is most probably not the ancient city on the Mediterranean coast of Turkey, but a place near to Shiheet where Saint Moses went to draw water *(Paradise,* Book 1, vol. 2, ch. 13, §619), which was his custom *(Paradise,* Book 1, vol. 2, ch. 13, §624). Petra could very well be a rocky crag in the solitude of the desert of Shiheet.

to himself, "How will I be able to get water here?' "fren an instruction of this sort came from above to him: "Enter, and be concerned for nothing." And so, he entered. Some fathers approached him, but he had nothing except a single flask of water, which was all used up after cooking up a little pot of lentils. This is why the old man was troubled. So, as he entered and departed he used to pray to God. And behold, a rain cloud came over Petra and filled all his vessels with rainwater. Thereafter they would urge the old man, saying, "Explain to us why you were going out and coming in." He answered them, "I was pleading my case with God, saying, 'You led me here, and behold, I lack water for your servants to drink.' Therefore, I used to go in and out begging God until He should send us water."

Lessons in Warfare [4]

The brethren said, "Why is it that though the holy fathers incite us continually to the labors of excellence, and to the contending against passions and devils, Abba Isidore restrained Abba Moses the Ethiopian from works, and from contests with devils, saying, 'Rest, Moses, and do not quarrel with the devils, and do not seek to make attacks upon them, for there is a measure moderation in everything, does this apply also to works and to the labors of the ascetic life?'"

The old man said, "Because at the beginning Abba Moses was ignorant of the rule of the ascetic life, and because he was healthy of body, he worked vigorously. He

---

'The notable connection with Abba Isidore suggests that This Abba Moses mentioned here is Abba Moses the Ethiopian.

[4] *Vitae Patrum,* Book II, §617.

thought that he would be able to prevail mightily against devils by the multitude of his works alone, and that he would be able to vanquish them. When the devils perceived his object, they attacked him more severely with frequent wars, both secretly and openly. So, Abba Isidore said to him, "Rest yourself, O Moses. Do not trouble yourself against the devils, and do not seek to make attacks on them. There is moderation in everything, even in the works of ascetic life." Then Moses said to him, "I believe in God, in Whom I have placed my hope, that being armed against the devils I must not cease to wage war with them until they depart from me." And Abba Isidore said to him, "In the Name of Jesus Christ, from this time forward the devils shall cease from you. Draw near, then, and participate in the Holy Mysteries, and you shall be free from all impurity both of the flesh and of the spirit. You must not boast within yourself, and say, 'I have overcome the devils,' for it was for your benefit that they have waxed strong against you."

So Moses returned again to his cell. After two months, Abba Isidore came to him and asked him concerning himself. Moses said to him, "I never see now anything which is hateful to me." But Abba Isidore, wishing to teach him the truth, and to make him to acquire humility, said to him, "Without the power of the Spirit which our Lord gave us in baptism for the fulfilling of His commandments—which is confirmed in us each day by the taking of His Body and Blood—we cannot be purified from the passions, we cannot vanquish devils, and we cannot perform the works of spiritual excellence."

Thereupon, Abba Moses learned these things, and his thoughts were humbled. He partook of the Holy Mysteries.

The devils were conquered, they reduced their war against him, and from that time onward he lived in rest, knowledge, and peace. Many monks imagined that their passions would be healed, and that they would acquire soundness of soul merely by their labors and strenuousness, and therefore they were abandoned by grace, and fell from the truth. But just as he who is sick in his body cannot be healed without the physician and medicines, not matter how much he may watch and fast during the time he is taking the medicine, so he who is sick in his soul through the passions of sin, without Christ, the Physician of souls, and without the partaking of His Body and Blood, the power which is hidden in His commandments, and the humility which is like His, one cannot be healed of his passions and cannot receive a perfect cure. Therefore, whoever fights against the passions and the devils by the commandments of our Lord is healed of the sickness of the passions, acquires health of soul, and is delivered from the crafts of the devils."

Early Battles in Petra[5]

Thereupon demons sprung on Blessed Moses (that is how we should call him), urging him to his habit of unbridled fornication. They tempted him to such a degree, as he himself recounted, that they were just short of being successful in dissuading him from his religious vows. He approached Isidore the Great, who was dwelling in Shiheet, and recounted to him for the third time of his war against fornication.

---

[5] It is most probable that this demonic attack occurred in the first years of the saint's life in solitude, perhaps before he began dwelling in Petra.

The holy man answered him, "Do not be alarmed, brother; these are just the initial stages. They have attacked you so intensely because they are seeking out an earlier pattern of habit. Indeed, it is just like a dog that is accustomed to gnaw on bones in the market; it does not change its habit. But if the market is closed, if no one gives him bones, he goes there no longer, since he is exhausted from hunger. So, too, if you persevere in your practice of continence, if you mortify your members which are upon the earth, if you prevent gluttony[6] from making its attack, the demon will take it ill and depart, seeing that it lacks food that sets you afire."

So, Christ's servant, Moses, departed. And from that hour, he shut himself up in his cell and practiced remarkable long-suffering in all trials. He especially practiced abstinence from food, such that he ate nothing except ten [or twelve] ounces of dry bread. He performed a great number of works and recited fifty prayers in full each day. Although he was making his body waste away into nothing, he yet continued to be intensely afire, chiefly in his dreams.[7]

Not even by these means did the holy solitary's tremendously intense struggle with the spirit of darkness cease, especially his dreams; it persisted on into the future with the utmost obstinacy, just as we learn from Palladius, who continues his account as follows:

"He got up and encountered another holy old monk who was of the utmost uprightness. He said to him, 'What am I to do, Abba? My dreams plunge my reason into darkness

---

[6] Gluttony produces lack of self-control.

[7] Palladius, pp. 63-64.

such that I should make of matters of one-time habit a source of pleasure.'

"The holy man said to him, 'You did not keep your mind from what you saw going on in the dreams. That is why you are undergoing this. So, do what I tell you. Devote yourself gradually to practicing night-watches, pray soberly, and you will be quickly delivered from these dreams.' When the noble man heard this advice as it were from the experience of a man who was an expert, he returned to his cell. He said that the whole night he did not sleep,[8] he did not bend the knee on the pretext of praying; his goal in so doing was to put to flight the tyranny of sleep.

"So, he spent six years in his cell; he stood in the middle of the cell night after night, prayed to God ceaselessly, did not shut his eyes, and yet was unable to defeat his disordered desire. In very point of fact, it is impossible for desire to be truly checked. He had reduced himself to a jelly with his toils and was yet unable to overcome that base inclination."

Those Who are with Us[9]

Once the demon of fornication waged war upon the blessed Abba Moses, who used to dwell in the place that used to be called Petra, such a fierce attack that the old man was unable to stay in his cell. He went off to the holy Abba Isidore and reported to him how violent was the attack. Abba Isidore produced for him texts in witness from Sacred Scripture to give him consolation. He asked him to return to his cell, but he was unwilling to make his way to his cell.

---

[8] An experience that he should know by personal acquaintance.

[9] *Vitae Patrum* 8.10, p. 494 ff.

[9] Sozomen, p. 682.

Then Abba Isidore accompanied Abba Moses to the upper level of his cell.

Isidore said to him, "Look to the West, and see." And he looked and saw a multitude of demons were in a state of violent, furious disorder, and, as it were, ready for battle, they were in a rush to do battle. Abba Isidore said to him, "Look, in turn, to the East, and see." He looked and saw a countless multitude of holy angels, the host of the heavenly powers, who shone with a glory greater than the light of the sun.

Abba Isidore said to him, "Behold, those whom you saw in the West are the very ones attack even the holy ones of God. Those on whom you gazed in the East are the very ones whom God sends to help His saints. Recognize, then, how very many are on our side, as the prophet Elisha says (cf. 2 Kings 6). Saint John also says, 'The One Who is in you is greater than the one who is in the world'" (1 John 4:4). Upon hearing these words, the holy Moses was strengthened in the Lord and returned to his cell. He gave thanks and glorified the long-suffering goodness of our Lord Jesus Christ.

The Holy Athlete[10]

From his former way of life he had acquired a healthy physique; it was yet a source of agitation and induced filthy, lustful thoughts. This being the case, he pummeled his body with every form of monastic discipline. He subsisted on a sparse ration of bread and abstained from cooked food. He performed extremely intense labors and prayed fifty times.

---

[10] Sozomen, p. 682.

From time to time he stood night after night and prayed for six hours unbroken, without bending his knees or closing his eyes to take some sleep.

Sometimes he went round at night to the cells of the monks and secretly filled their water pots with water. This was, in fact, a particularly toilsome task. The place where he drew water was ten stadia distant from some hermitages, from others twenty, and from others sometimes thirty and more stadia.[11] For a long time he retained his original hardiness despite his zealous efforts to break it through a vast number of forms of monastic discipline and his wearing down his body with intense hardships.

No Rest for the Righteous[12]

Following these occurrences he suggested to himself another manner of leading a harsh life. This man who boxed with Satan[13] went out at night and used to go off to the cells of the monks who had grown old in the toils of the monastic life and were unable to carry water back any longer by themselves. He took their water pots without their knowledge and filled them with water. Indeed, in those locales they have their water source at specific distances. Some were two miles away; some, five miles; others, half a mile.

So, one night when he was doing this the demon that had watched him could tolerate the athlete's fortitude no longer. When Moses bent over at the well to fill a monk's

---

[11] 10 stadia = 1.25 miles; 20 stadia = 2.5 miles; and 30 stadia = 3.75 miles.
[12] Palladius, pp. 65-66.
[13] In fact, Abba Moses struggled with him in a variety of ways, as discussed below.

water pot, the demon struck his loins with a staff and left him lying there dead, utterly senseless of what had happened to him or who had done it. On the next day a monk came there to draw water and found him lying there in a swoon. He reported this to Isidore the great, the priest of Shiheet.

Isidore went off with some other [monks], picked him up, and brought him to the church. For a whole year he was ill, the outcome of which was that his body and soul recovered their health with difficulty. Then the priest of Christ, the great Isidore, said to him, "Brother Moses, stop struggling with the demons, and do not scoff at them so. For there is a limit to one's strength in monastic discipline." But he said to him, "I will never cease battling them until the images in my dreams stop." Then the holy priest Isidore said to him, "In the Name of our Lord Jesus Christ your filthy dreams have ceased from this very moment. Come, then, and receive the Mysteries with confidence and a clear conscience.[14] Indeed, lest you boast that you overcame this feeling by your own practices, this is why he had such great power over you. It was for your own good, lest you should fall into a prideful attitude."

---

[14] The words, "Receive the Mysteries with confidence and a clear conscience," could mean that the saint felt weakened from the seething ferocity of his temptations, that he either did not receive the Sacraments or at least that he did not do so μετά παρρησίας,, as we read in Palladius' Greek text, i.e., with freedom, with boldness (we should not say "freely" or "boldly"). Moreover, it is not credible that our saint abstained from the Mysteries for the six full years that this struggle against the flesh lasted. Second, it seems plausible that he might receive the Mysteries, yet less frequently than other monks, that he regarded himself unworthy to receive them too frequently owing to holy dread, a great sense of awe that he felt.

Once Moses heard this he returned to his cell and then tranquilly practiced a moderate program of monastic discipline. Two or three months later blessed priest Isidore asked Moses the Athlete whether the spirit still bothered him. He answered, "From the hour that the servant of Christ prayed for me, nothing like that has occurred."

The Source of the Passions[15]

Abba Moses said, "Passion arises by means of these four things: by means of an abundance of food and drink, by means of taking sufficient sleep, by means of having free time and joking, and by going about in finely decorated clothing."

The Defeat of the Passions[16]

He said, "The body has many passions." And the brother said to him, "What are they, Abba?" He answered, "The Apostle Paul says, 'But fornication and all uncleanness or all covetousness, let it not even be named among you, as is fitting for saints' (Ephesians 5:3); reliance on one's power of sight, too, frequently engages one in battle."

Acknowledge Your Sin [17]

Abba Moses said, "If the monk does not think in his heart that he is a sinner, God will not hear him." The brother asked him, "What does that mean, 'to think in his heart that he is a sinner?'" Then the old man said, "When

---

[15] *Vitae Patrum*, 3.58, p. 510.

[16] *Vitae Patrum*, 7.1.7, p. 665.

[17] *Ascetical Writings to Poemen*, Moses, 3.

someone is occupied with his own faults, he does not see those of neighbor."

How to Overcome Temptation[18]

The old man was asked, "What should a man do in all the temptations and evil thoughts that come upon him?" The old man said to him, "He should weep and implore the goodness of God to come to his aid, and he will obtain peace if he prays with discernment. For it is written, 'The Lord on my side, I will not fear. What can man do to me? (Psalm 118:6).'"

A Life of Weeping[19]

In the desert of Shiheet [c. 390],[20] where the most tried and true monastic fathers dwelt, one could see complete perfection in company with the holy Abba Germanus. There, I sought out Abba Moses, who was an ardent practitioner of the practical and contemplative life. I was eager to be grounded by his instruction...Together we wept profusely and petitioned the same old man for a word to edify us, since we recognized all too well his steadfastness of spirit, that he would not in any way at all agree to share insight into the doctrine of perfection except with those who desire it with faithfulness, who seek it with complete, heartfelt contrition. Otherwise, the risk would obviously be that in relating vital matters indiscriminately to those who do not in fact desire it, who are lukewarm in seeking it, matters that ought be disclosed only to those who seek

---

[18] *Ascetical Writings to Poemen,* Moses, 6.

[19] Cassian, *Collationes,* 1.1, p. 174.

[20] *Ibid.,* p. 72.

perfection, he would be yielding to men who are unworthy of this doctrine, men who would receive it scornfully, and it would seem ostentatious vice on his part, or that he was blameworthy of a crime of betrayal of trust.

Conquering Boredom (Acedia)[21]

When I began living in the desert, I told Abba Moses, the greatest of all the holy men living there, how the day before I was completely and utterly spent from the affliction called *acedia* and how I was unable to free myself from it other than by rushing straightaway to Abba Paul. He replied, "You have not freed yourself of it; rather, you have demonstrated that you have given in to it and are subject to it. Indeed, the enemy will attack you much harder as a deserter and runaway, one whom he saw bested in the conflict and at once running off. Thus, when the battle is joined anew, you must resolve to make his heated assaults go up in smoke when his hour comes. This will not happen by deserting your cell or being groggy with sleep. On the contrary, it is by long-suffering and by engaging in the conflict that you will learn to defeat this." Thus, this experience has proven that we must not flee, we must not yield to the attacks of *acedia*; we must resist and overcome them.

Become Like the Dead[22]

A brother questioned Abba Moses saying, "I see something in front of me and am unable to get hold of it." The old man said to him, "Unless you become dead like those who are sealed in the tomb, you will be unable to take

---

[21] John Cassian, *De institutis coenobiorum*, 10.25, p. 142.
[22] Cotelier, p. 558.

hold of it."

The Life of the Tomb[23]

Abba Poemen said that a brother asked Abba Moses, saying, "What sort of man is dead to himself or towards his neighbor?" He answered him, "If a man does not think in his heart that he has already spent three days in the tomb, he does not attain this saying."

Blessed are You When They Revile You[24]

The brethren said, "Abba Moses the Ethiopian was on one occasion reviled by certain men, and the brethren asked him, saying, 'Was not your troubled in your heart, O father when you were reviled?' And he said to them, 'Although I was troubled, yet I spoke not.' What is the meaning of the words, 'Although I was troubled I spoke not?'"

The old man said, "The perfection of monks consists of two parts, that is to say, of impassibility of the senses of the body, and of impassibility of the senses of the soul. Impassibility of the body takes place when a man who is reviled restrains himself for God's sake and speaks not, even though he is troubled. But impassibility of the soul takes place when a man is abused and reviled, and yet is not angry in his heart when he is abused, even like John Colobos.[25] For on one occasion when the brethren were sitting with him, a man passed by and rebuked him, but he was not angry, and

---

[23] *Vitae Patrum*, 5.10.63, p. 602.

[24] *Paradise*, Book II, §669.

[25] Abba John Colobos is Abba John the Short (or Dwarf). The word "colobos" comes from the Coptic for stoutness or short stature.

his countenance did not change. Then the brethren asked him, saying, 'Are you not secretly troubled in your heart, O father, being reviled in this fashion?' And he answered and said to them, 'I am not troubled inwardly, for inwardly I am just as tranquil as you see that I am outwardly.' And this is perfect impassibility."

Now at that time Abba Moses had not arrived at this state of perfection, and he confessed that although outwardly he was undisturbed, yet he was waging a contest in his heart, and he maintained silence and was not angry outwardly. And even this was a spiritual excellence, although it would have been a more perfect thing had he not been angry either inwardly or outwardly.

And the blessed Nilus made a comparison of these two measures of excellence in the cases of the blessed men Moses and Aaron. The act of covering the breast and heart with the priestly tunic which Aaron performed when he went into the Holy of Holies represented the state of a man who, though angry in his heart, suppresses his wrath by striving and prayer; and the state of a man not being angry at all in the heart, because he has been exalted to perfection by his victory over the passions and the devils, Nilus compared to that which is said of the Blessed Moses, saying:

"Moses took the breast for an offering, because the soul dwells in the heart, and the heart in the breast and Solomon said, 'Remove anger[26] from your heart' (Ecclesiastes 11:10). Concerning Aaron, the Book says, 'He was covering his breast with the ephod and tunic.' This teaches us monks that it is meet for us to cover over the wrath which is in the heart

---

[26] Alternatively, "sorrow."

with gentle, humble, and tranquil thoughts, and that we should not allow it to ascend to the opening of our throat, because the odiousness and abomination thereof shall be revealed by the tongue."

V

A LIFE OF VIRTUE

Our blessed saint did not proffer his instructions on perfection wantonly and fruitlessly. He wanted to pass them on to those who were eager for them, who sought them with a contrite, humble heart, lest they do them harm, should they not have the proper disposition.

When Palladius and others were compiling the sayings and stories of the *Apophthegmata*, they came across many small collections that may have served as models to their work.[1] Among these was a document entitled, *Seven Headings of Ascetic Conduct*, which was believed to have been written by Abba Moses and sent to Abba Poemen.[2] The preface reads, "He who puts them into practice will escape all punishment and will live in peace, whether he dwells in the desert or in the midst of brethren."[3] Some of these are included below. Once again, we assume that this Abba Moses is the same as Moses of Ethiopia, although this cannot be entirely substantiated.

---

[1] William Harmless, *Desert Christians: An Introduction to the Literature of Early Monasticism* (New York: Oxford University Press, 2004), p. 205.

[2] *Ibid.*

[3] *Ibid.*; Cotelier, pp. 368-69.

The Humble Priest[4]

They used to say of Abba Moses that he became a member of the clergy and they placed the ephod[5] upon him. The archbishop said to him, "Behold, Abba Moses, you have hereby become dazzlingly white." He answered, "You think so of the outside, my lord papa,[6] but do you think it of the inside?" Wishing to test him, the bishop said to the clergy, 'When Abba Moses enters the sanctuary, drive him out, and follow him to hear what he says.' When they began driving him out, they kept on saying to him, 'Get out, Ethiopian!' But as he departed, he said, 'They have done you a kindness, man of ash and soot. Seeing that you are not a man, so why would you dare present yourself among men?'"[7]

Obey the Fathers [8]

At Shiheet Abba Moses used to say, "If we keep the commandments of our Fathers, I will answer for it on God's behalf that the barbarians will not come here. But if we do not keep the commandments of God, this place will be

---

[4] *Vitae Patrum* 5.15.29, p. 624. In the Vitae Patrum is treated Saint Moses' priesthood, which was proven through the holy man's profound humility as he retreated into the shadows of modesty and abjection.

[5] The term ἐπωμίς is generally rendered as "ephod." The Coptic rite terms *sedrah,* and the Byzantine rite calls the *epitrakhelion* or *phailonion.*

[6] Reference here to title of respect given to the Patriarch Theophilus of Alexandria.

[7] Rosweyde observes the following on the words rendered "man of ash and soot" in the Vedastinus and Audomarensis manuscripts. Some variant editions read, "man covered in ash and soot" or "man made of ash and soot." It seems that the word rendered 'of ash' is qualitatively the same as 'dusty' and the like.

[8] *Sayings of Abba Moses of Shiheet.*

devastated."

Humility Humbles Demons [9]

He was obedient to their requests and he would say, "Brethren and fathers, humility humbles demons and vainglory elevates them. Whoever is humble and speaks humbly is able to neutralize demonic power, but whoever does not have humility becomes the toy of the demons. Whoever prays, if he does not believe that he is a sinner, will not be heard by our Lord. Nor will He receive his prayer. One must always have before him all his sins and seeing these impure actions clearly, he will not judge anyone else at all."

Labor and Toil [10]

These are the words which Abba Moses said to Abba Poemen. And the first word, which was spoken by the old man, was: "It is better for a man to put himself to death rather than his neighbor, and he should not condemn him in anything. It is good for a man to die to every work which is evil, and he should not trouble a man before his departure from the body."

Labor and Prayer [11]

Abba Moses said, "If a man's deeds are not in harmony with his prayer, he labors in vain." A brother asked him, "What is this harmony between practice and prayer?" The

---

[9] *Ibid.*

[10] *Paradise,* Book II, ch. 1, §119-121.

[11] *Ascetical Writings to Poemen,* 4; Harmless, p. 205, fn. 54.

old man said, "We should no longer do those things against which we pray. For when a person gives up his own will, then God is reconciled with him and accepts his prayers. It is written, 'God is our refuge and strength, a help in the afflictions that have come heavily upon us'" (Psalm 46:1).

The Hardships of the Soul[12]

The old man was asked, "What is the good of fasts and watchings which a man imposes on himself?" And he replied, "They make the soul humble. For it is written, 'Look upon my affliction and my trouble, and forgive all my sins' (Psalm 25:18). So if the soul gives itself all this hardship, God will have mercy on it."

Examine Your Faults[13]

A brother asked the old man, "Here is a man who bears his servant because of a fault he has committed; what will the servant say?" The old man said, "If the servant is good, he should say, 'Forgive me, I have sinned.'" The brother said to him, "Nothing else?" The old man said, "No, for from the moment he takes upon himself responsibility for the affair and says, 'I have sinned,' immediately the Lord will have mercy on him. The aim in all these things is not to judge one's neighbor. For truly, when the hand of the Lord caused all the first-born in the land of Egypt to die, no house was without its dead." The brother said, "What does that mean?"

The old man said, "If we are on the watch to see our

---

[12] *Ascetical Writings to Poemen, 5.*

[13] *Ascetical Writings to Poemen, 7.*

own faults, we shall not see those of our neighbor. It is folly for a man who has a dead person in his house to leave him there and to weep over his neighbor's dead. To die to one's neighbor is this: To bear your own faults and not to pay attention to anyone else wondering whether they are good or bad.

"Do no harm to anyone; do not think anything bad in your heart towards anyone; do not scorn the man who does evil, do not put confidence in him who does wrong to his neighbor; do not rejoice with him who injures his neighbor. This is what dying to one's neighbor means.

"Do not speak out against anyone, but rather say, 'God knows each one.' Do not agree with him who slanders; do not rejoice at this slander; and do not hate him who slanders his neighbor. This is what it means not to judge.

"Do not have hostile feelings towards anyone; do not let dislike dominate your heart; and do not hate him who hates his neighbor. This is what peace is.

"Encourage yourself with this thought, 'Affliction lasts but a short time, while peace is forever, by the Grace of God the Word.' Amen."

Work and Pray[14]

Abba Moses used to say, "Secret withdrawal from work makes the mind dark. But enduring to persevere in his works makes enlightens the mind in our Lord. Thus, it strengthens and fortifies the soul."

---

[14] *Paradise,* Book I, vol. 1, ch. 6, §227.

Judge Not, Lest You be Judged[15]

A certain brother committed an offense in Shiheet, the camp of the monks, and when a congregation was assembled on this matter, they sent after Abba Moses, but he refused to come. Then they sent the priest of the church to him, saying, "Come, for all the people are expecting you." So he rose up and came. He took a sack with a hole in it and filled it with sand, and carried it upon his shoulders, and those who went out to meet him said to him, "What does this mean, O father?" And he said to them, "The sands are my sins which are running down behind me and I cannot see them, and, even, have come to this day to judge shortcomings which are not mine." And when they heard this they set free that brother and said nothing further to him.

Extreme Humility[16]

Once a provincial judge heard about Abba Moses, and he headed to Shiheet to see him. Some people reported to the old man about his coming; he got up to flee to the marsh. The judge and his retinue met him and asked him, saying, 'Old man, tell us; where is Abba Moses' cell?' He said to them, 'Why do you seek him? He is a fool and a heretic.'

So the judge went to the church and said to the clergy, "I heard about Abba Moses and went to see him; behold, an

---

[15] *Paradise*, Book I, vol. 2, ch. 10, §542; *Vitae Patrum* 5.9.4, p. 594. Together with the virtue of charity, mercy has no small affinity towards those who have fallen in sin. The holy man exhibited that he showed mercy in a degree exceeding the other brothers who inhabited the wilderness, for the latter wished to punish a brother who was guilty of some fault; the former, however, wished to have him spared.

[16] *Vitae Patrum*, 5.16.7, p. 631.

old man heading to Egypt met us, and we asked him where Abba Moses' cell was. He said to us, 'Why do you seek him? He is a fool and a heretic.'" When the clergy heard this, they were grieved and said, "What kind of an old man was that who said to you these things about the holy man?" They said, "An old man wearing very old clothes, a tall black man." They said, "He was Abba Moses himself; he said these things to you about himself because he did not want you to see him." The judge departed greatly edified.

The Host of Angels[17]

A brother came to Shiheet and asked to see Abba Arsenius. Some brothers tried to persuade him to rest a little. He answered, "I shall not eat bread unless I get to meet him." Then one of the brothers led him to Abba Arsenius. He knocked on the doorway to the cell and led him in. Once they were welcomed and had said a prayer they sat down. Blessed Arsenius remained silent. The brother who had led the other brother there said, "I am leaving." But the brother who had had such great desire to come noticed that Abba Arsenius had said nothing to him; he felt ashamed and was sitting in silence, too. He said, "I am also leaving you." And so they both departed. The visitor also asked him to take him to Abba Moses, who had converted from being a robber. He welcomed them, showed them charity, and sent them on their way.

The brother who had brought him to both old men said to him, "Behold, you have seen both old men whom you asked to see; which of the two do you prefer?" "Presently I prefer the one whom we saw last who gave us such a good

---

[17] *Vitae Patrum*, 7.18.2, p. 673; *Paradise*, Book 1, vol. 2, Ch 1, §21.

welcome and fed us." When word of this got out, one of the fathers prayed to the Lord, saying, "Lord, please show me the meaning of this matter: for one for Your Name's sake flees from seeing anyone and does not even say the name of anyone; the other, for Your Name's sake, is hospitable with everyone." Behold, in a vision two boats were shown to him on a river. In one he saw the Spirit of God sailing in silent tranquility with Abba Arsenius; in the other he saw Abba Moses and the angels of God eating honey and honeycomb in great mouthfuls.

Fasting with Love[18]

From this virtue resulted the following undertaking of our holy father: I believe that he preferred to seem less rigid in his observance of a fast rather than to show too little hospitality when some solitaries arrived. The account of what happened is written up as follows:

"Once an order was given in Shiheet that they should fast that week and celebrate the Pascha.[19] It happened that brothers came from Egypt to Abba Moses in that very week. He made them a moderate quantity of food. His neighbors saw the smoke and said to the clergy of the church there, 'See, Moses has broken the commandment and has cooked food in his cell.'" The former said, 'When he comes, we will speak to him.' When Saturday came, since the clergy knew Abba Moses' noble way of life, they said to them in front of

---

[18] *Vitae Patrum*, 5.13.4, p. 615; *Paradise*, Book I, vol. 2, ch. 9, §441.

[19] This demonstrates the ancient custom of a one-week fast for the Feast of Holy Resurrection, which seems to date to the time of St Moses in the fourth century. Also, the Feast of the Resurrection was referred to as *Pascha,* or the Passover.

the whole company, 'O Abba Moses, you broke the commandment of men, but you steadfastly kept the commandment of God.'"

Four Principles of Life[20]

Abba Moses was attempting to impress upon the brethren the following, "A monk has four principal works to observe: to keep silent, to keep God's Commandments, to humble himself, and to experience the want proper to being poor. Therefore, to mourn always, a monk must always be mindful of his sins and have death always before his eyes."

In His Own Words[21]

I prefer your salvation in the fear of God above all things, asking Him to make you complete in pleasing Him, so that your effort is not to waste, but acceptable to God with joy and gladness...For we know that merchant is pleased when his business is successful. Also, one who learns a trade is pleased when he becomes proficient in his trade, forgetting the effort, because he reached the proficiency he desired. Also, one who marries a woman who keeps her reputation has pleasure that fills his heart. And one who

---

[20] *Vitae Patrum*, 3.196, p. 529. These four principles are in reasonable agreement with those that we read in book seven of the *Vitae Patrum*, 7.35.1, p. 680.

[21] William A. Hanna, "The Remembrance (Martyrdom) of 'Anba Moussa Al-Assouad': Saint Moses the Black, 24th of Baonah, July First." Saint Louis, MI: Saint Mary & Saint Abraam Coptic Orthodox Church, 2003), pp. 8-9; trans. from His Grace Bishop Andraous of Blessed Memory. Saint *Moses the Black* (in Arabic). Apparently, Saint Moses wrote the following to Abba Poemen. 'the following is slightly modified.

attains the honor of military service will not fear death in the fight against the enemies of his king to please his master. Every one of those mentioned is pleased to achieve his goal and strives to attain it.

If this is so for the things of this world, how much more will soul that chooses to serve God succeed in pleasing Him? Truly, I say to you that its pleasure is greater, because at the time of its departure, its good deeds meets her there. The angels are pleased when they witness her release from the powers of the darkness, because when the soul leaves the body is accompanied by the angels. It is then met by the powers of the enemy who try to hinder it because of what it owes them. The angels, then, have no business to try to defend it, but only its good deeds can defend it and protect it from its accusers. And when its victory is complete, the angels rejoice over that soul. They then praise God with it until it meets the Lord with gladness. At that moment, it forgets all the sorrows of this world.

So, our way, my dear friend, is to exert the maximum effort in the short time we have on earth; to correct and purify our deeds from all evil. We hope to attain salvation by the Grace of God from the hands of the devils who are anxious to meet us, especially if any of their works are in us-- for they are evil and show no mercy. So, blessed is the soul that is free from them, it will be pleased and her pleasure is great.

For this reason, my dear friend, we have to strive with tears so that the Lord may, in His kindness, have mercy on us. For "those who sow with tears shall reap with exceeding joy" (Psalm 125:5). Let us posses the desire to be with God, because those who desire God protect themselves from the desire to commit adultery. And those who desire meekness protect themselves from the love of silver. Let us desire peace to protect ourselves from hatred. Let us posses patience and long-suffering which will protect us from pettiness of the soul. Let us posses pure love for all, which will protect us from envy and jealousy. Let us be humble in every act and every deed. Let us tolerate being cursed and ridiculed to purge ourselves of pride. Let us be kind to all our neighbors to avoid condemnation. Let us reject the glories of the world and its honors to avoid false pride. Let us use the tongue to glorify God and to protect ourselves from lying. Let us love purity of heart so we may be saved from corruption. All of these things surround the soul and follow it when it leaves the flesh.

If anyone is wise and works with wisdom, let him surrender the spirit without possessing those good deeds that will assist him to pass through the difficulty. So, let us be as careful as we can, so that the Lord will help our weaknesses. Because the door of forgiveness is always open to those who repent as long as we are in the flesh.

His Gift of Prophecy[22]

There was a certain old man in Shiheet who, having become very sick indeed, was ministered to by the brethren. When he thought in his mind that they were tired of him, he said, "I will go to Egypt, so that the brethren may not have to labor on my account." But Abba Moses said to him, "You shall not go, for if you go you will fall into fornication." The old man was grieved and said, "My body has long been dead, and you say these things to me?" So he went up to

---

[22] *Paradise,* Book I, vol. 1, ch. 35.

Egypt. When men heard about him, they brought many offerings to him, and a certain believing virgin came in faith to minister to him. After a time, when the old man had been healed, the young woman lay with him. When she conceived, the people asked her, saying, "From whom have you conceived?" And she said to them, "From the old man," and they did not believe her.

Now when the old man heard that they would not believe her, he said, "Yes, I have done this thing, but protect for me the child which shall be born." After the child had been born and was weaned, when there was a congregation in Shiheet, the old man would enter into the church before the people, while carrying the child on his shoulder. And when they saw him they all wept. Then the old man said to the brethren, "Observe, O my brethren, this is the child of disobedience. Take heed, then, to yourselves, for I have committed this act in my old age. Pray for me." And the old man went to his cell, and dismissed the things with which he had lived, and returned to his former deeds. After a time, he arrived once more at his old measure of ascetic excellence.

The Gates of Heaven[23]

Abba Poemen said: Abba Moses asked Abba Zechariah a question when he was about to die, saying, "Father is it good that we should hold our peace?" And Zechariah said to him, "Yes, my son, hold your peace." And at the time of his death, while Abba Isidore was sitting with him, Abba Moses looked up to heaven and said, "Rejoice and be glad, O my son Zechariah, for the gates of heaven have been opened."

---

[23] *Paradise*, vol. 2, ch. 1, §31.

VI

HIS DEPARTURE

As mentioned above and in the Abyssinian metrical hagiography, Abba Moses is believed to have been martyred with six other anchorite martyrs, by a tribe of barbarian raiders, the Mazices, who attacked Shiheet from the Libyan Desert.[1] After examining the details of these martyrs alongside that of the other Moses and his six martyr companions, the extensive study of the Bollandists concluded they are the same. While John Cassian does not mention this raid, Saint Augustine writing in 409[2] refers to it as a well known event. Also, Philosotorgiu[3] places it during the reign of Arcadius (before 1 May 408).

An Account of His Martyrdom[4]

On one occasion when the brethren were sitting with

---

[1] See *Acta Sanctorum,* June 3, p. 586, commentary for June 18; Harmless, p. 205.

[2] cf. Epist. 111 in PL 33:422.

[3] *Hist. Eccl.,* 11.3. Philosotorgius (368 - ca. 439) was a Anomoean Church historian of the fourth and fifth centuries. He was born in Cappadocia, lived in Constantinople, and wrote a history of the Arian controversy

[4] *Paradise,* Book II, ch. 1, §45; *Apophthegmata Patrum,* Theodore of Phereme, 26.

Abba Moses, he said to them, "Behold, this day has the barbarians come to Shiheet; rise up and flee." And they said to him, "Will you not flee, father?" He said to them, "I have been expecting this day to come for many years past, so that might be fulfilled the command of our Redeemer, 'All who take the sword will perish by the sword'" (Matthew 26:52). And they said to him, "Then, we will not flee, but will die with you." He said to them, "This is not my affair, but your own desire. Let every man look after himself in the place where he dwells." Now the brethren were seven in number. And after a little he said to them, "Behold, the barbarians have drawn near the door." And the barbarians entered and slew them. Now one of them had been afraid, and he fled behind the palm leaves, and he saw seven crowns descending and being placed on the heads of those who had been slain.

Ⲇⲟⲝⲁ ⲥⲓ ⲟ̀ Ⲑⲉⲟⲥ ⲏ̀ⲙⲱⲛ

VII

DOXOLOGY TO THE STRONG

ABBA MOSES

Ⲡⲓϣⲟⲣⲡ ⲙ̅ⲙⲁⲣⲧⲩⲣⲟⲥ ⲉⲑⲟⲩⲁⲃ:
ⲉ̀ⲧⲁϥϫⲱⲕ ⲉ̀ⲃⲟⲗ ⲛ̅ⲕⲁⲗⲱⲥ:
ϧⲉⲛ ⲡⲓⲧⲱⲟⲩ ⲛ̅ⲧⲉ Ϣⲓϩⲏⲧ:
ⲡⲉ ⲡⲉⲛⲓⲱⲧ ⲉⲑⲟⲩⲁⲃ ⲁⲃⲃⲁ
Ⲙⲱⲥⲏ.

Ⲁϥϣⲱⲡⲓ ⲅⲁⲣ ⲛ̀ⲟⲩⲣⲉϥϯ: ⲉϥⲟⲓ
ⲛ̀ϩⲟϯ ⲟⲩⲃⲉ ⲛⲓⲇⲉⲙⲱⲛ: ⲁϥⲟ̀ϩⲓ
ⲉ̀ⲣⲁⲧϥ ϩⲓϫⲉⲛ ϯⲡⲉⲧⲣⲁ: ⲕⲁⲧⲁ
ⲡ̀ⲧⲩⲡⲟⲥ ⲙ̀ⲡⲓⲥ̀ⲧⲁⲩⲣⲟⲥ.

Ⲃⲓⲧⲉⲛ ⲧⲉϥⲛⲓϣϯ ⲛ̀ϩⲩⲡⲟⲙⲟⲛⲏ:
ⲛⲉⲙ ⲡⲓϭⲓⲥⲓ ⲛ̀ⲧⲉ ⲛⲓⲃⲁⲥⲁⲛⲟⲥ:
ⲁϥⲉⲣⲫⲟⲣⲓⲛ ⲙ̀ⲡⲓⲭ̀ⲗⲟⲙ: ⲛ̀ⲧⲉ
ϯⲙⲉⲧⲙⲁⲣⲧⲩⲣⲟⲥ.

Ⲁϥϩⲱⲗ ⲉ̀ⲡ̀ϭⲓⲥⲓ ϧⲉⲛ
ⲡⲓⲡ̀ⲛⲉⲩⲙⲁ: ⲉ̀ϧⲟⲩⲛ
ⲉ̀ⲛⲉϥⲙⲁⲛ̀ⲉⲙⲧⲟⲛ:
ⲉ̀ⲧⲁϥⲥⲉⲃⲧⲱⲧⲟⲩ ⲛ̀ϫⲉ Ⲡϭⲟⲓⲥ:
ⲛ̀ⲛⲏⲉⲑⲙⲉⲓ ⲙ̀ⲡⲉϥⲣⲁⲛ ⲉⲑⲟⲩⲁⲃ.

The first holy martyr, who was truly perfected, on the mountain of Shiheet, is our holy father Abba Moses.

He became a fighter, whom the demons fear, he stood upon the rock, a type of the Cross.

Through his great patience, of the pain of the sufferings, he wore the crown, of martyrdom.

He flew in the spirit to the heights, to His place of rest, which the Lord has prepared, for those who love His holy Name.

Ⲁϥⲥⲱϫⲡ ⲛⲁⲛ ⲙ̀ⲡⲉϥⲥⲱⲙⲁ:
ⲛⲉⲙ ⲡⲉϥⲥⲡⲏⲗⲉⲟⲛ ⲉⲑⲟⲩⲁⲃ:
ⲉⲑⲣⲉⲛϫⲱⲕ ⲉ̀ⲃⲟⲗ ⲛ̀ϩⲏⲧϥ:
ⲙ̀ⲡⲉϥⲉⲣⲫⲙⲉⲩⲓ ⲉⲧⲧⲁⲓⲏⲟⲩⲧ.

Ⲉⲛⲱϣ ⲉ̀ⲃⲟⲗ ⲉⲛϫⲱ ⲙ̀ⲙⲟⲥ: ϫⲉ
Ⲫⲛⲟⲩϯ ⲛ̀ⲁⲃⲃⲁ Ⲙⲱⲥⲏ: ⲛⲉⲙ
ⲛⲏⲉ̀ⲧⲁⲩϫⲱⲕ ⲉ̀ⲃⲟⲗ ⲛⲉⲙⲁϥ:
ⲁ̀ⲣⲓⲟⲩⲛⲁⲓ ⲛⲉⲙ ⲛⲉⲛⲯⲩⲭⲏ.

Ⲟⲩⲟϩ ⲛ̀ⲧⲉⲛϣⲁϣⲛⲓ ⲉ̀ⲛⲓⲱϣ:
ⲉ̀ⲧⲁϥⲥⲉⲃⲧⲱⲧⲟⲩ ⲛ̀ⲛⲏⲉⲑⲟⲩⲁⲃ:
ⲉ̀ⲧⲁⲩⲣⲁⲛⲁϥ ⲓⲥϫⲉⲛ ⲡ̀ⲉⲛⲉϩ:
ⲉⲑⲃⲉ ⲧⲟⲩⲁ̀ⲅⲁⲡⲏ ⲉ̀ϧⲟⲩⲛ
ⲉ̀ⲣⲟϥ.

Ⲧⲱⲃϩ ⲙ̀ⲡ̀ϭⲟⲓⲥ ⲉ̀ϩⲣⲏⲓ ⲉ̀ϫⲱⲛ:
ⲱ̀ ⲡⲁϭⲟⲓⲥ ⲛ̀ⲓⲱⲧ ⲁⲃⲃⲁ Ⲙⲱⲥⲏ:
ⲛⲉⲙ ⲛⲉϥϣⲏⲣⲓ ⲛ̀ⲥⲧⲁⲩⲣⲟⲫⲟⲣⲟⲥ:
ⲛ̀ⲧⲉϥⲭⲁ ⲛⲉⲛⲛⲟⲃⲓ ⲛⲁⲛ ⲉ̀ⲃⲟⲗ.

He left for us his holy body, and his holy cell, that we may be perfected, in his honored remembrance.

Proclaiming and saying, "O God of Abba Moses, and those who were perfected with him, have mercy upon our souls."

That we may win the promises, which He has prepared for the saints, who have pleased Him since the beginning, because of their love for Him.

Pray to the Lord on our behalf, O my father Abba Moses, and his children the cross-bearers, that He may forgive us our sins.

BIBLIOGRAPHY

Apophthegmata Patrum.

Augustine. *Epistle 111.* PL 33:422.

His Grace Bishop Andraous of Blessed Memory. Saint *Moses the Black.*

Hanna, William A. "The Remembrance (Martyrdom) of 'Anba Moussa Al-Assouad': Saint Moses the Black, 24th of Baonah, July First." Saint Louis, MI: Saint Mary & Saint Abraam Coptic Orthodox Church, 2003.

Bulteau, Louis. *Histoire de l'ordre monastique.*

Callistus, Nicephorus. *Ecclesiasticae historiae.*

Cassian, John. *Collationes.* Lyons, 1606.

_____. *De institutis coenobiorum.*

Cotelier, Jean-Baptiste. *Ecclesiae Graecae Monumenta.*

Coquin, Rene Georges. "Etudes sur Moise d'Abydos." *Annuaire de l'Ecole pratique des Hautes Etudes, Ve section, Sciences religieuses* (1983/84): 373-376.

_____. "La 'Regle' de Moise d'Abydos," *Cahiers d'Orientalisme* 20 (1988): 103-110.

_____. "Moise d'Abydos," *Deuxieme journee detudes coptes, Cahiers de la bibliotheque copte* 3 (1986):1-14.

Gazet, Alard ed., *Collationes 1: Joannis Cassiani opera omnia.* Paris: 1642.

Harmless, William. Desert Christians: *An Introduction to the Literature of Early Monasticism.* New York: Oxford

University Press, 2004.

Ludolf, Job. *Fastis Sacris Ecclesiae Aethiopicae.*

Moussa, Mark. "The Coptic Literary Dossier of Abba Moses of Abydos." *Coptic Church Review* 24:3 (2003):66-90.

_____. "Abba Moses of Abydos." MA Diss, Catholic University of America, 1998.

Palladius. *Historia Lausiaca.*

_____ *Vita abbatis Dioscuri presbyteri.* trans. Gentenian Hervet. PG 34. 1579.

Poemen. *Ascetical Writings,* ed. Rosweyde.

"Saint Moses the Ethiopian: Hermit, Abbot, and Perhaps Martyr at Mt. Scetis in Libya, Introduction and Commentary." *Acta Sanctorum,* August VI, pp. 199-209.

Sozomen. *Historia ecclesiastica.* Trans. Henri Valois. Paris, 1668.

Tillemont. *Monumentorum ecclesiasticorum.*

Vitae Patrum. Trans. by Heribert Rosweyde.

Ward, Benedicta. *The Desert Fathers: Sayings of the Early Christian Monks.* London: Penguin Books Ltd, 2003.

Made in the USA
Middletown, DE
09 September 2023

38234561R00046